# You Might Be a ~~Crazy~~ Dedicated Hockey Dad If . . .

Jason Howell

*illustrated by Braden Howell*

Magenta Entertainment Ltd.

Library and Archives Canada Cataloguing in Publication Data

Howell, Jason, 1967-
    You Might Be a ~~Crazy~~ Dedicated Hockey Dad If . . .

ISBN 978-0-9687692-1-8

1. Hockey — Humour. 2. Fathers — Humour. 3. Father and child — Humour. I. Title

PS8565.0873Y68 2012     C813'.54     C2012-904829-1

Printed and bound in Canada

Magenta Entertainment Ltd.

This book is dedicated to my youngest son, Myles.

Kid, this is probably as good a time as any to tell you: I've kind of been buying more pucks every now and again, so that "set of 100" you've been shooting in the backyard every day — in all honesty, it's been more like 200, lately. I regret not telling you earlier, but regret even more that we're not doing 300.

—J.H.—

# INTRODUCTION

As a hockey dad, you've endured the early morning practices, the long car drives (sometimes through blinding snow storms), and the re-financing of your house to pay for extra power skating lessons. You are, indeed, a survivor, someone who gives 110% (unlike some of the players on your kid's team!). And now you've decided to "take it up a notch" by reading this book, which is chock-full of HOCKEY SECRETS GUARANTEED TO HELP YOUR PLAYER ACHIEVE HIS (or your) GOAL OF PLAYING IN THE NHL.

If you're a little "crazy," you're no different than the rest of us. We'll do "whatever it takes," because we love our kids . . . we love them and just want them to do BETTER than Bill's kid, you know the one, AAA Johnny down the street.

I must confess, at this point, that I stand (or sit) before you now as someone particularly well qualified to be writing on this subject (ie., a little crazy), and am an ideal target for SOME of the jokes here. I have spent hours strategizing for a Tyke game; cut back on groceries, so we could pay for more power skating; lied about my boy's age to get him into a higher-level camp; built a synthetic ice rink in my backyard; snuck out of work early to make it to out-of-town games — and this was all in the early years! What a trip it's been, though! Throughout my kids' minor hockey careers, there's nothing I have looked forward to more than the "games on the weekend." I mean, life is short — pass my kid the puck already!

I do need to emphasize, though, that these jokes are "all in good fun." I am not, in any way, condoning the behavior of the over-the-top parent who berates their kid, their coach, the referee, or another parent. That's not cool. We all understand this, and yet all of us, even the best of us, have said and done things, "in the heat of the moment," that could register a little higher than we'd like on the "crazy meter." Sometimes, all we need is a humourous perspective to remind us where "the line" is — and (hopefully) this book offers just that.

# Pre-Game (Psycho) Analysis

Our hockey-dad experiences are usually shaped and determined, for better or worse, by our player's skill level and ranking in the overall "pecking order." What does this mean? Generally speaking, if your kid is a star player, the other dads will find you — and bring you coffee; but if your kid is a below-average player, you'll only hear these dads (yelling "helpful" suggestions from the stands) — and you'll be avoided like a future rectal exam.

What you might not realize, though, is that most hockey dads fall into 1 of 6 basic types. Understanding the type (and corresponding testosterone level) of the dad you're dealing with (or who's charging towards you) can give you and your player a competitive advantage as the season moves forward. Master these types and it will be: Psychology 1, Psycho Hockey Dad 0.

# A Field Guide to Hockey Dad Types

# HOLY GLASSBANGER DAD!
## (Volcanus InterEruptus Dad)

# GLASSBANGER HOCKEY DAD

Game-day characteristics:
- Stands by the glass (often alone) at all games.
- Turns head sideways to yell at the team through cracks in the glass.
- Kicks boards with feet and pounds glass with hands simultaneously, . . . and hovers in the air like a crazed hummingbird while performing this maneuver.

Range and habitat:
- Lives at the corner glass area (and has no idea where wife or partner actually sits during games).
- Legend of when he last erupted is enough to keep others at a comfortable distance.

Diet
- Coffee, coffee, and more coffee.

Communication skills:
Expresses himself through grunting and Morse Code-like glass-banging . . . 3 bangs and you should be running.

# I Believe I Can Coach . . . Clipboard Dad
## (Lupiter Nemesis Pater)

# CLIPBOARD HOCKEY DAD

## Game-day characteristics:

- Gives personal, detailed instructions to his player (and all within hearing distance) outside the dressing room before games.

## Range and habitat

- Through some quirk of fate, this dad was assigned placement in the stands instead of his rightful place behind the bench.
- Often sits directly behind the bench area, and tells everyone what he would do if he were the coach.

## Diet

- No time to eat.

## Life cycle and mating

- Spends most of his free time (to his wife's delight!) deciding whether or not he should "go for the team next year."
- Wife is a saint.

# What Time is it Mr. . . . Stopwatch Dad?
## (Chronos Irritatus Pater)

# STOPWATCH HOCKEY DAD

## Game-day characteristics
- Whereas most "hockey beings" exist in both time and space, this dad mainly exists in time (and outer space).
- Keeps track of his player's ice time with a not-so-secret stopwatch.
- Can be relied on to offer helpful hints like, "The clock is still running!" or "Just drop the puck already!"
- Keeps all the players' stats (without being asked to).

## Range and habitat
- Sits in the stands, where he can "count time," camouflaged among other fans.

## Diet
- Tums and Pepto-Bismol.

## Life cycle and mating
- Has been overheard to tell Clipboard Dad that he "completes" him.

# I am the Warrior . . . Dad
## (Mars Victorius Pater)

# WARRIOR HOCKEY DAD

## Game-day characteristics:
- Have you ever seen Braveheart? Well, so did Warrior Dad — only 10 times more than you did.
- He believes in a "physical game," and offers up ear-splitting (and terrifying) battle cries like, "Take the body!" and "Hit someone!"
- Finds it "disgraceful" when a kid lies on the ice hurt (and thinks concussions are "way over-diagnosed").

## Range and habitat
- Often in the middle of multiple wars on multiple fronts.
- Will sometimes stand with Glassbanger Dad or sit with the kids who are hurt or suspended.

## Diet
- Gatorade and a full dose of testosterone.

## Life cycle and mating
- Summer is mating season (after playoffs, of course).

# The Legend of Invisible Dad
## (Insula Injustus Pater)

# INVISIBLE HOCKEY DAD

## Game-day characteristics:
- He stands alone, in the far corner of the rink, a veritable Robinson Crusoe (with no man Friday).
- He comes in the back door; leaves through the back door.
- He does not shout or draw attention to himself in any way.

## Range and habitat
- Outside the rink? Unknown.

## Diet
- Chews the bitter cud of previous injustices.

## Life cycle and mating
- Not exactly a joy to be around, he will generally move further down the glass if he sees someone coming (and is highly attuned to the placement of all exits).
- Only Warrior Dad seems to remember when Invisible Dad was still visible.

# I Am Always Drunk Dad
## (Bacchus Labbattus Pater)

# ALWAYS DRUNK HOCKEY DAD

## Game-day characteristics:

- This throwback to old-time hockey understands that it's not about skill-building or winning — it's about getting together for a few "pops" afterwards . . .
- His main question in life is, "Does this arena have a bar?"
- Ironically, he is completely okay with the whole "team concept idea," mainly because he's completely disinterested in the actual team.

## Range and habitat

- Arena-bar viewing area.

## Diet

- Beer and beer nuts.

## Life cycle and mating

- Keeping this hockey dad well fed, well watered (and well laid (with the "right" partner) — these are the keys to having a successful hockey season.

# You Might Be a ~~Crazy~~ Dedicated Hockey Dad If...

- You secretly get a little giddy when a player on your kid's team gets hurt or suspended, because you know it'll mean more ice time for your kid.

- You've told your kid to skate beside the weaker players, so he'll look better in try-outs.

- The last book you read was your hockey association's rules and by-laws manual.

You're always looking for
"teachable moments" at the dinner table.

# You Might Be a ~~Crazy~~ Dedicated Hockey Dad If...

- You've given your player strict instructions to do crossovers whenever there's a break in the play, because you want to "get your money's worth."

- You had his first skates bronzed.

- It's a consistent pattern every Christmas: your family spends the holidays together, while you spend most of the time in the back yard building a rink your kids don't really want and won't ever use.

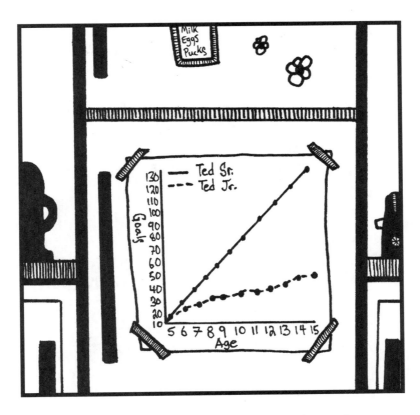

You've graphed your player's point production versus your own at his age as a "motivational tool."

# You Might Be a ~~Crazy~~ Dedicated Hockey Dad If...

- You've bribed the arena staff so your kid could stay out longer after practice.

- The first word you free-associate with "budget" is "team" rather than "family."

- You find yourself parked in the first (and best) arena parking space at 6:01 a.m.; your kid is already fully dressed and ready to go on the ice; and you're upset that the arena maintenance guy hasn't shown up yet.

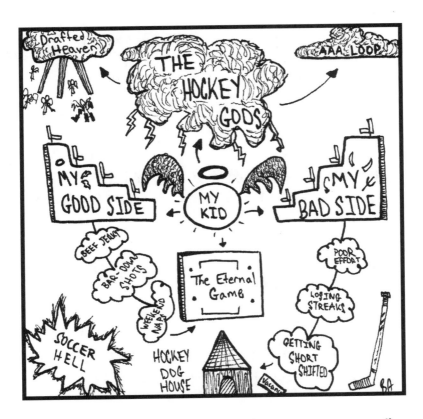

You not only believe in "hockey karma,"
but have actually started to worship the
"Hockey Gods."

# You Might Be a ~~Crazy~~ Dedicated Hockey Dad If...

- The school calls and asks why little Bobby is wearing training weights on his ankles and wrists in kindergarten class.

- You list your player's stats separately — on his own website.

- You've asked the coach to plan the team's schedule around your kid's private training.

Just the sight of certain patterns is
enough to set you off.

# You Might Be a ~~Crazy~~ Dedicated Hockey Dad If...

- You've spent a lot of time developing a secret, fool-proof strategy for your kid to win at British Bulldog.

- If another parent ever complains about the "excessive amount of ice time lately," you move away from them, quietly labeling them as "crazy."

- Even the mother of your children won't sit beside you at the games.

Everyone can't help but agree that, as a fan, you give "110% effort every game."

# You Might Be a ~~Crazy~~ Dedicated Hockey Dad If...

- The coach has told you he's "keeping you on a short leash this year."

- You find yourself taking pre-game naps, drinking energy drinks, and planning your entire day around your kid's one hour of ice time.

- You've told your wife that your job is getting in the way of seeing the kids' games . . . and she's had to remind you about the whole paying-off-the-mortgage thing.

Secret team meetings have been held not
only without you, but about you.

# You Might Be a ~~Crazy~~ Dedicated Hockey Dad If...

- Your wife tells you she's leaving for good, and you ask if there's any way she can wait until after the hockey season, because you're concerned it might be "disruptive to the team's chemistry."

- You've spent hours calling around to see what extra ice times are available for the team — and you're not even the manager.

- Your opinion on who should play goal is old school — fat kid.

The coach actually expects to have to talk to you after each and every game.

# You Might Be a ~~Crazy~~ Dedicated Hockey Dad If...

- It's your 4-year-old's first time on skates, but it's already clear to you that "he lacks focus and drive."

- Your jacket pockets are always overflowing with tennis balls, weighted-hockey balls, golf balls, Green Biscuits, and energy bars.

- The introduction-to-the-team letter comes with a list of vocabulary substitutions the team would like you to entertain when yelling this year.

You buy all your pucks by the dozen.

# You Might Be a ~~Crazy~~ Dedicated Hockey Dad If...

- You get excited (and sometimes offer up a fist pump) when your kid scores in warm-up.

- You've told your player exactly who he can and can't pass the puck to.

- You find yourself requesting pre-game urine samples from players who look "just too damn big."

You're sometimes overcome by an irresistible urge to "coach from the stands."

# You Might Be a ~~Crazy~~ Dedicated Hockey Dad If...

- You and your player are both off with suspensions at the same time.

- You drink your coffee the same way each game: double-fisted.

- You've told the coach he can play your little skater wherever he sees fit . . . except on defence . . . or on the wing.

You encourage your kids to listen to the soothing (and motivating!) sounds of "crossbar dings" before bed.

# You Might Be a ~~Crazy~~ Dedicated Hockey Dad If...

- You act surprised when told "there are other players on the team."

- You let your 8-year-old watch Slapshot, because you consider it "educational."

- You've stopped trying to relive your childhood dreams through your kid, mainly because you've completely forgotten you're actually 2 different people.

You're spending most of your time "pretending to live somewhere else" to meet the "residency requirements."

# 1st Period Intermission

## FUNDRAISING FIASCOS...

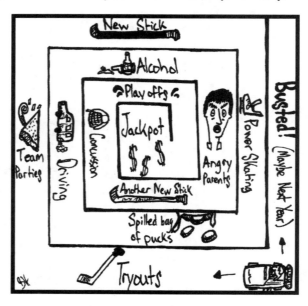

Take a break, relax, grab a beer . . . and then check out the best (or worst?) Hockey Fundraising Ideas.

Midget AA Bottle Drive
Regina, SK
Photo: ~~1923~~ Last Week

# Who's in the Can? 50/50

## An Idea Donated by Marty Shitzer
## (Prince Albert, SK)

This 50/50 draw can done at any time in the season, and is fun for all ages. Simply wait in the lobby, before or after a game, until most of your team's parents are milling about. As soon as someone from your group goes into a lobby washroom, quickly pull up a table and chair in front of the washroom doors, barring anyone from the possibility of escaping.

A 50/50 confederate then starts yelling, "Who's in the can? Who's in the can?" At the same time, a 2nd confederate quickly blindfolds everyone (so they can't figure it out by process of elimination). Then, the 1st confederate takes down guesses, at $15 per guess. Now, I should add, at this point, that even though the table and chair are flush with the washroom doors, the person in the can might still try to escape. In fact, after hearing all the commotion, they might be quite desperate to get out. It is imperative that they be kept in the can at all costs. Make up a convincing story: tell them there's a fire in the arena, and they'll be safer near all the water in the washroom. Do what you have to do . . .

When all the guesses have been made, you ask people, with the rising inflection of a circus performer, "Would you like to know who's actually in the Can?" "Yes, yes," they scream . . . "Please tell us who is in the can, for we can wait no longer."

Then, with much theatrics, you swing open the washroom door, exposing any and all inside.

A variation on this theme is the "Who's in the Arena Bar 50/50." This can be more tricky, though, as most people are often already in the bar.

Fundraising target: $150

# The Congenital Stone Hands Charity

## An Idea Donated by Murray "Medusa" Smith
## (Badlands, AB)

It is a little-known fact that 1 in 3 Canadians suffer from Congenital Stone Hands. These poor creatures lack the basic ability to move the puck down the ice with any kind of fluency or grace. And give them an open net —they'll shoot the puck in the rafters. It's so sad . . . and they need your help!

Aligning your group's fundraising efforts with a charity like this is a great way to enhance public awareness of the affliction, while at the same time raising money for treatment (more ice time).

Simply identify 2 or 3 players on the team who suffer from CSH, and ask them to stickhandle some pucks while on prominent display in a downtown shop's store window. Add a homemade sign asking for donations for "Kids with

Stone Hands," and, trust me, the money will start rolling in. Keep your head up, Juvenile Diabetes!

The Stone Hands Campaign is also a good experience for the kids singled out: it helps them understand their own limitations, and to realize that, though they are doing nothing on the ice (at least nothing positive), they can still make contributions to help the better players on the team.

Fundraising target: $1500

# The Book Burning "Deal"

## An Idea Donated by Guy Montag
## (St. Laurent, QC)

If you have spent any time at all in arenas, you have probably spotted "parent readers," perched high up in the stands. Every team has one or two of these rare birds, who can't be coaxed out of their books come hell or high water. Thinking they're still in high school, studying away for some departmental exam that will never come, they choose to bury their noses in books — rather than gossip and complain like the rest of us.

They're also often the last ones to help out with fundraising, which led me to this idea: just go over, grab their book, and threaten to throw it into the fire unless they donate $5 to the team's coffers (you'll need to have started a small fire beforehand). They'll almost always pay up, as the book is worth more than $5 (so it's a deal to get it back for that price — at least, that's the way I see it).

They're still wavering? Maybe complaining a little about not having cash on hand, or not wanting to pay the ATM fee? Here's where I hit them in the solar plexus by flipping through their book and reading out randomly chosen excerpts, like this one, in front of all the other parents:

". . . Peter was big and muscular (not unlike a work horse). He moved towards her. His left eye twitching spasmodically. Her mind went blank . . . grey, actually, like the many shades of grey of his pant pockets . . ."

"Heard enough, Bookworm Mom? Then, pay up!"

Works every time!

Fundraising target: $5

# Tell-Us-What-You-Really-Think Valentines

## An Idea Donated by Peter Hart
### (Conception Bay, NFLD)

There's nothing more stressful than going through an entire season without being able to tell the parents and coaching staff what you really think of them. The pent-up rage can be enough to cause hockey parents to spontaneously combust mid-season.

Open the emotional floodgates and relieve the pressure this Valentine's Day by launching the Tell-Us-What-You-Really-Think Valentine's promotion.

You simply cut heart shapes out of multi-coloured construction paper, and then sell them for $5 each. The buyer writes down what they really think of another parent or coach, and then the team delivers this "constructive criticism" to its intended target.

The beauty of this is that, not unlike an email war, after the first shot has been fired, another is sure to follow . . . and your team's fundraising committee is nicely positioned as the exclusive "battlefield messenger."

And here's a tip to get this fundraiser rolling: if business is a little slow at first, and people aren't quite getting into the holiday spirit, you can always "step up" and "fire the first shot."

Fundraising target: $2000

# Referee Box Lunch

## An Idea Donated by Gary "Offside" Hunter
## (Vancouver, BC)

Have you ever wondered why anyone would want to become a hockey referee? Well, you might not know that it's all based on one thing: failing your eye test. If instead of seeing alphabetic letters, you see things like "hooking" and "high-sticking" — stuff that isn't even there — consider yourself enrolled in ref school . . .

Anyone who fails the eye test at a young age is removed from general society, and brought up by wolves in the Canadian wilderness — to strengthen them for the hardships they will suffer years later on the ice. At the age of 12, they are re-introduced to their families and encouraged to "apprentice" as timekeepers, only after rigorous testing confirms they are completely incompetent at posting penalty minutes correctly on the scoreboard. Finally, at the age of 14, they are taken to the horse races, and whoever consistently misreads which horse crosses the finish line first is then "promoted" to call offsides as a hockey linesman.

Luckily, you don't need that little history lesson to run the Referee Box Lunch fundraiser. You just need to invite all the referees in town to your next social event — tell them they will be well fed and honoured for their on-ice contributions — and then auction off a box lunch with each of them. Don't be surprised if your parents show a great deal of enthusiasm for the idea: they'll quickly identify a ref who called a penalty on their kid 10 years ago, and pay $50 to find out "Why the hell that call was made?"

It's fun for the referees as well, as they don't spend nearly enough time talking to the "chirping" parents in the stands.

Fundraising target: $5000 (allow for beefed-up security costs).

# Congratulations — It's a Divorce!

## An Idea Donated by Teddy Singleton
## (Keswick, ON)

On any hockey team, it's normal for the players, parents and siblings (even with all the different personalities and often conflicting interests) to become very close — like an extended family, in fact. And it can be very difficult (and awkward) for all involved when one of the families goes through an divorce.

On one particularly close-knit team, the manager decided to get a little more involved in the divorce process, and the team asked for custody of their star player (they were concerned he might miss games and practices). With the next divorce, the team started looking to participate in an even bigger way: the manager acted as divorce lawyer for the tidy sum of $1500. Assets were split using the eenie-meenie-miney-moe method, and anything of real value went to the team to compensate for the disruption.

They also instituted a policy — and this seems to have been unique to this group — that once a couple has filed for divorce, the other parents receive a "free pass" to sleep with one of the new singles. It just adds a bit of fun to what can otherwise be a dull and divisive year of hockey.

A variation on this theme is the "Hello, I'm Your Doctor!" fundraising campaign, where you take someone with no medical training and send them out on actual life-and-death emergencies. Some confusion could arise here, however, as there is clearly overlap with this idea and the role of hockey trainer.

Fundraising target: $3000 (and unlimited gossip).

# The Santa Letters

## An Idea Donated by Little Mike
## (Bracebridge, ON)

Do your kids write Santa a letter every Christmas? And does his reply usually arrive sometime in early February? That was our experience. Our kids would just stare, bewildered, when Santa's reply letter would finally arrive. Santa can deliver the presents all around the world in one night, but it takes him an entire month to deliver a letter? What's up, Santa? And what's this reference to "eating our cookies?" We didn't leave out any cookies . . . Now it looks like he's not only breaking into our house, but also rooting through our cupboards as well? Alarm bells (or the need for better ones) started going off . . .

Our team got fed up with Slacker Santa's turnaround time, so we decided to write our own reply letters. They've been a huge hit (and now arrive on time). Here's how it works: your team sets up a Santa PO Box, and then sells the Santa Letter Writing Program to friends and family for $30. The children mail the letters, and then the parents follow up, secretly, with a personalized "Naughty or Nice Profile."

The first year we ran the program we made a profit of $4000. But then, admittedly, we got a little greedy. Why stop at writing letters? we asked ourselves. And so the next year, we implemented a Santa Home Placement Program, where, for $250, we would place a Santa on your roof (bell sounds included). You want your kid to see him "running through the woods"? An extra $50. You get the picture.

What we didn't count on was that we now had so many Santas on any given street that kids were looking out their windows and seeing 2 or 3 Big Reds (sometimes on the same roof). What makes matters worse, some enterprising Santas took it upon themselves to run off with all the presents . . .

Fundraising target: $4000 (but keep your Santas off the rooftops).

# Timmy's Run

## An Idea Donated by Bobby "Double-Double" Miller
## (Cold Lake, AB)

According to the latest medical research, 70% of a hockey dad's body is comprised of Tim Horton's coffee. Startling figures. I was actually surprised, after seeing all the Timmy's runs over the years, that the numbers weren't higher. Let's go for 100% was my thought — and that's how the Timmy's Undercoffee Run was born.

We rented the local swimming pool, had it drained, and then filled with Tim Horton's coffee (double-double in the deep end). Spectators were charged a gate fee of $10 to watch the parents flounder about for the day, while all involved were charged $1.80 for every large cup-full they managed to scoop out of the pool. Races were also held at the beginning — mostly to see who could get out of the pool fastest (before they were completely scalded).

In retrospect, I would highly recommend that participants wrap themselves in cardboard sleeves before jumping in, as — I'm not going to lie to you — many in our group suffered severe burns (and filed lawsuits). We didn't raise much money, that's true, but we all took a little comfort in the knowledge that we now had a season's worth of emergency coffee swilling around in the back of Toby's truck.

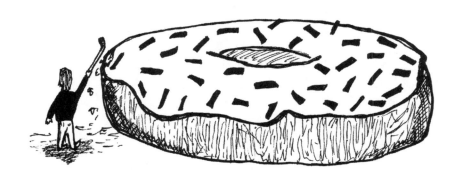

Fundraising target: free coffee (and giant doughnuts!)

# You Might Be a ~~Crazy~~ Dedicated Hockey Dad If...

- Your personal grudges are "ancient history" — meaning, biblical in proportion and destined to be repeated.

- You had first pick in the Fantasy Hockey Pool, and you chose your own kid.

- After all these years, you've finally figured out how to bang-out free snacks from the arena vending machines.

You've taught your kid to apply everything
he's learned from hockey to the
work world.

# You Might Be a ~~Crazy~~ Dedicated Hockey Dad If...

- It's become apparent to everyone at work that you just can't concentrate on game days; unfortunately, it's also become apparent that just about every day is game day.

- You're spending so much time driving to away games that you've started to fantasize about the nice (though slightly bossy) lady on your GPS.

- You keep track of your player's stats in 3 on 3.

You make a "Timmy's run" just for the coach (and don't need to ask "how he takes it").

# You Might Be a ~~Crazy~~ Dedicated Hockey Dad If...

- Your main concern about the afterlife is whether or not you can bring your stick.

- You've had more concussions in the stands than the kids have had on the ice.

- It's cold outside, it's the weekend, and you have the no-hockey-again-today shakes.

You've got creative solutions for
weekend scheduling conflicts.

# You Might Be a ~~Crazy~~ Dedicated Hockey Dad If...

- It's not uncommon for you to complain loudly in the stands about the "stupid decisions THAT KID makes" within hearing distance of THAT KID'S parents.

- You've asked the coach (on more than one occasion) to see the game sheet to double-check your player's stats.

- You've looked into taking out insurance on your player's "extra-soft hands."

Your hockey-volunteer work has become more time-consuming than a full-time job.

# You Might Be a ~~Crazy~~ Dedicated Hockey Dad If...

- You've pulled your player from school to take advantage of non-prime ice rates.

- You thought "Rock 'em, Sock 'em" was part of the Hockey Canada Skills Program.

- You've declined a significant promotion at work, because the new job would interfere with your kid's hockey schedule.

You have definite opinions about how (and at what speed) the ice should be cleaned.

# You Might Be a ~~Crazy~~ Dedicated Hockey Dad If...

- The guys at work actually expect an unedited play-by-play of your kid's games come Monday morning.

- You think Don Cherry should be consulted on matters of foreign policy.

- You've demanded passionately that the 10-year-old operating the score board needs "to put those 5 seconds back on the clock immediately."

Dear Bobby Orr,

I really enjoyed watching you play for the Bruins in the "good ol' days." Maybe you remember me? I wrote you a letter 40 years ago asking for an autographed picture. Anyway, thanks for the memories (I never did get that picture).

As an aside, do you still have good connections in the OHL? My son, Bill Jr., is lighting it up this year in Novice. He's scored 53 goals in 28 games so far — all from the back end. He's a rushing "D" just like you were, Bobby! No worries, though, Bill Jr.'s knees are actually good. They say the pros make everything look easy — it sure didn't look easy when you flew through the air after scoring that OT playoff goal against St. Louis. Bill Jr. would have tucked it in neatly, and then skated quickly back to centre. Anyway, let us know what the scouts are saying about our boy, and it's never too late to send me that picture.

Billy (Tunnel Vision) Williams

You talk about your kid all the time, but that's not bragging — it's just good PR.

# You Might Be a ~~Crazy~~ Dedicated Hockey Dad If...

- You show up to tournaments fully prepared — dressed in "beer pants."

- You've "cut out the middle man," and now simply pay the coach for your kid's goals.

- There's a new arena security policy named after you.

You've started to book conflicts with opposing teams' parents in advance, so you're "better organized" this season.

# You Might Be a ~~Crazy~~ Dedicated Hockey Dad If...

- The voices in your head are telling you the team should pass the puck more.

- You've asked if there's any way the weaker kids on the team can be traded.

- The other player always seems to "turn at the last minute," just before your kid hits them from behind.

You buy the optional trading cards every season, even though the team photos are free.

# You Might Be a ~~Crazy~~ Dedicated Hockey Dad If...

- You consider arena poutine a "breakfast food."

- Your kid has an agent — and he's only in Tyke.

- You pay for everything in cash (so it doesn't leave a paper trail), and you (wisely) neglect to tell your better half exactly how much you paid for certain pieces of equipment.

You're completely aware that your player can't hear you yell — that's why you use sign language.

# *2nd Period Intermission*

## ANGRY OSTRICH INC. PRESENTS . . .

### THE BEST HOCKEY PRODUCTS
### FOR PEOPLE WHO HAVE WAY TOO MUCH MONEY

### <u>WALKIE JOCKIE 3000</u>

Ever feel that your mid-game advice to "Skate!" and "Shoot!" is falling on deaf ears? Concerned that the coach's instruction might be over-riding your own coaching from the stands?

With the new Walkie Jockie 3000, a revolutionary hockey-headset technology, you can now holler your advice directly into your player's helmet. It comes complete with a full set of instructions to yell in different scenarios. Order today, and receive a coach-jammer device at no extra charge.

You call the shots now . . . with the Walkie Jockie 3000!

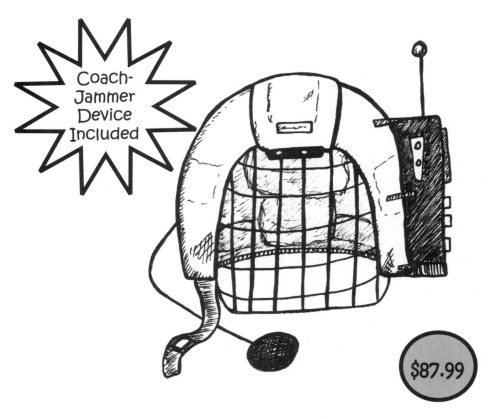

Coach-Jammer Device Included

$87.99

79

# INSTANT HOCKEY HANDS CREAM

Tired of fans yelling, "Go home, Stone Hands" every time your player has the puck? Pulling your hair out over countless open-net opportunities that go unconverted?

With new Instant Hockey Hands Cream, your player will be blessed with hands that feel like (and are now worth) a million bucks. Simply apply once, and wait for the scouts to call (don't even bother taking him to practice).

IHHC — created from a secret formula that includes a rare combination of ground Chinchilla and cobra venom extract — works to disconnect the hands from the central nervous system and brain (the biggest obstacle to a player's development).

## Oh, so soft . . . and then they strike!

Available at hockey stores everywhere.

**STONE HANDS BE GONE!!**

Dangle more than just your participles this season . . .

$19.87

Instant Hands

The only thing standing between your player and the NHL is you (and your current indecisiveness). Act now and get a free container for the coach's kid — let's face it: that kid needs all the help he can get!

# MASTER PUPPETEER
# COACH STRINGS

For many hockey parents, they know someone's pulling the coach's strings, but they can never actually see it in action. Now, not only will you be able to see the strings — you can be the one pulling them! With Master Puppeteer Coach Strings, you can control the coach's every move from your place in the stands.

For no extra charge, we'll also send Assistant-Coach-in-a-Box. Wind it up, and, well, he'll just stay in the box forever, so terrified is he of the parents.

Available exclusively at stringemup.ca

# STRING 'EM UP TODAY WITH

# MASTER PUPPETEER COACH STRINGS!

REAL TESTIMONIAL:

". . . on our team, let's just say we got a little tired of watching the coach play his own kid all the time. We thought about staging a coup, but lacked the energy (and Pete kept forgetting the tar and feathers). After implementing the MP Coach Strings Program, Coach does what we want . . . and we're all a lot happier.

Placated in Pickering

# ROSE-COLOURED SPORT'S GLASSES

Distracted by all the other players who, let's be honest, just make it more difficult to see your own? Wanting to drink the coach's "Kool-Aid," but unable to keep it down?

With our new RCS Glasses, complete with side blinders to block out "unimportant players," everything will look rosy again in no time. Also, with our patent-pending FKM TECHNOLOGY, the glasses filter out pre-programmed images of people you don't like. No longer will you have to avoid them at the rink — you won't even see them anymore.

Finally, for an extra $10 per month, your glasses can feature a 2-second image delay, assigning your player's jersey number to anyone who does anything good on the ice.

Find out more at allaboutmyownkid.com

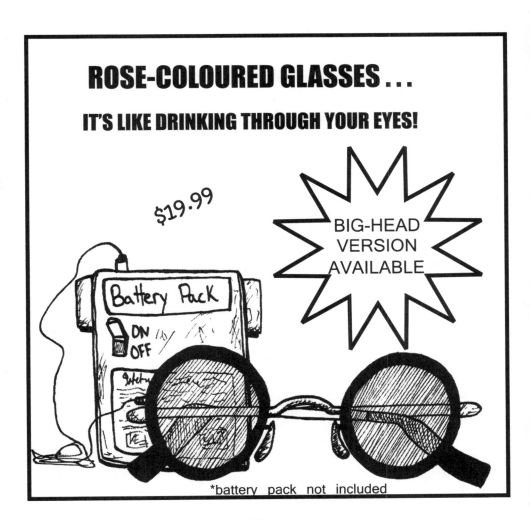

# The 24-Hour Ruler

Wanting to talk to the coach about your player's ice time, but never quite sure how to apply his "24-Hour Rule?" Like many hockey parents, it might not be clear to you when the 24-hour period would actually start and stop (especially because you're almost always upset about something).

With our new 24-Hour Ruler, you simply hold it up when angry, giving "fair notice" to everyone at the rink that you will be calling the coach in 24 hours. No one will ever be confused again.

And what if you forget? The ruler will ding like an egg timer, telling you when the coach is done.

Available for a limited time (24 hours!) at timetotalk.ca

# IT TICKS . . .

## IT TOCKS . . .

## THEN YOU

# EXPLODE!

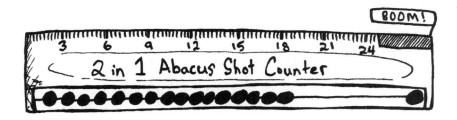

NO MONEY DOWN . . . AND WE'LL DO ANYTHING TO
PLEASE YOU!

# You Might Be a ~~Crazy~~ Dedicated Hockey Dad If...

- Everyone wants to talk to your wife instead of you.

- At tryouts, the evaluator's notes gloss over your kid and focus on you.

- You like your drinks and have been invited to an AA meeting, but you refuse to go because you know AAA is better.

You're seeing a therapist about your ice-time addiction.

# You Might Be a ~~Crazy~~ Dedicated Hockey Dad If...

- You've tried to move a wedding date (or a funeral) because it conflicts with a "big game."

- Your wife's talked to you about it, but you just can't see the point . . . I mean, Bobby Clarke never needed braces.

- When someone tells you that "referees are human, too," you debate this.

Your kid's team has an assistant coach
with only one responsibility —
you!

# You Might Be a ~~Crazy~~ Dedicated Hockey Dad If...

- You freak out the entire family because you're running late for a game (and that's "unacceptable") only to find yourselves the first ones at the rink.

- You are not on the bench, but, for whatever reason, you were in the team picture.

- When your name is mentioned, people just laugh . . . nervously.

All future communications with the coach must now go through your lawyer.

# You Might Be a ~~Crazy~~ Dedicated Hockey Dad If...

- You don't want to mention names, but you can (and you will) clearly identify those individuals responsible for today's loss.

- You think bodychecking should be introduced in Initiation.

- It's sometimes difficult to watch the game when standing beside you, because your heavy breathing fogs up the glass.

# THE 10 COMMANDMENTS OF HOCKEY DADS

1. Thou shalt not skate in front of thine own net (and just how many times do I have to keep saying that?).
2. Thou shalt listen to thy coaches — as long as they're on the same page as me.
3. Thou shalt have fun . . . immediately!
4. Thou shalt not slash another player . . . but I'll look the other way if it's "payback."
5. Thou shalt not hit from behind . . . but we all know kids are coached to turn at the last second to draw a penalty.
6. Thou shalt not steal . . . my kid's points from the game sheet.
7. Thou shalt not turtle — and you can't have one as a pet either . . .
8. Thou shalt not play goalie (it's too expensive!).
9. Thou shalt not put another sport before hockey — even lacrosse.
10. Thou shalt not covet thy neighbour's rink — just ask to use it!

# You Might Be a ~~Crazy~~ Dedicated Hockey Dad If...

- You could talk for hours (and sometimes do) about the "lost art" of skate sharpening.

- You collect errant pucks from out-of-town rinks to help maintain your supply.

- You've trained your player to sneak in the back door of arenas to avoid paying for public skating.

For some reason that even your family
doesn't understand, you made the
decision to become a referee.

# You Might Be a ~~Crazy~~ Dedicated Hockey Dad If...

- You've taught your kid to look both ways before he crosses the street, but you're totally okay with him playing road hockey in the middle of traffic.

- You encourage the "egging on" of opponents as a "necessary trait of an elite athlete."

- The Convenor has a file folder exclusively dedicated to your printed-out emails.

You've taken up yoga on the suggestion of your hockey-anger-management counsellor.

# You Might Be a ~~Crazy~~ Dedicated Hockey Dad If...

- Your post-game review often takes longer than the actual game.

- When you *see* construction pylons on the road, you can't help but weave your vehicle through them.

- You've found a top-notch power skating and skills program — and then kept the information to yourself.

You routinely buy equipment for your
player before he actually needs it.

# You Might Be a ~~Crazy~~ Dedicated Hockey Dad If...

- You've considered applying for a job at the rink, just to get consistent access to the ice-booking schedule.

- You find yourself craving arena hot dogs in the middle of summer.

- You chose your new vehicle based on the number of hockey bags it could hold.

You've never been shy about telling everyone who should "start in goal today."

# You Might Be a ~~Crazy~~ Dedicated Hockey Dad If...

- The coach takes player role call . . . and you answer.

- You've been asked to leave a friendship tournament.

- At the end of each month, you total up the number of hours your player was on the ice (and it's never quite enough).

You've implemented numerous player incentives simultaneously (even if they are complicated and contradictory).

# *3rd Period Time-out*

# WE WANT YOU . . .

## TO JOIN US ON NETWORK 55
### (THE SOCIAL NETWORKING SITE FOR HAPPY, FULFILLED SPORTS DADS)

| | |
|---|---|
| Anonymous<br>*(no login)* | **Network 55**<br>**Re: 2002 Stuffitville try-outs**<br><br>Any surprises for the 2002 Stuffitville try-outs this year? 11:32<br><br><small>No score for this post. Scoring disabled. You must be drunk to score posts.</small> |
| Anonymous<br>*(no login)* | Coach is the same guy who threw his gum at the ref in playoffs last year. 11:45<br><br><small>No score for this post. Scoring disabled. You must be drunk to score posts.</small> |
| Anonymous<br>*(no login)* | What kind of gum? 11:53<br><br><small>No score for this post. Scoring disabled. You must be drunk to score posts.</small> |
| Anonymous<br>*(no login)* | Mints are a better choice sometimes. 12:13<br><br><small>No score for this post. Scoring disabled. You must be drunk to score posts.</small> |
| Anonymous<br>*(no login)* | I remember the story: this clown got a GM-21 for a 5 game sit in the stands. 12:53<br><br><small>No score for this post. Scoring disabled. You must be drunk to score posts.</small> |
| Anonymous<br>*(no login)* | Worse still, I hear he throws like a girl. 3:10<br><br><br><br><br><small>No score for this post. Scoring disabled. You must be drunk to score posts.</small> |

| | |
|---|---|
| Anonymous<br>*(no login)* | **Network 55**<br>**Re: 2002 Stuffitville try-outs cont'd**<br><br>At least he's got some passion . . . our coach has never been kicked out of a game – not even once. 4:15 <br>No score for this post. Scoring disabled. You must be drunk to score posts. |
| Anonymous<br>*(no login)* | Probably left more gum under the bleacher seats, too. 5:13 <br>No score for this post. Scoring disabled. You must be drunk to score posts. |
| Anonymous<br>*(no login)* | What about the kids in the try-outs?  How do they look? 6:10 <br>No score for this post. Scoring disabled. You must be drunk to score posts. |
| Anonymous<br>*(no login)* | There are kids? 7:03 <br>No score for this post. Scoring disabled. You must be drunk to score posts. |
| Anonymous<br>*(no login)* | No worries, everyone.  I already picked the team for the coach.  Emailed him the list as well, and posted all on Facebook. 7:10 <br>No score for this post. Scoring disabled. You must be drunk to score posts. |
| Anonymous<br>*(no login)* | Good work, 7:10.  Nice to see there's still helpful parents out there. 7:15 <br><br>No score for this post. Scoring disabled. You must be drunk to score posts. |

| | |
|---|---|
| Anonymous<br>*(no login)* | **Network 55**<br>**Re: Should a kid be allowed to miss playoffs to go on vacation?**<br><br>No score for this post. Scoring disabled. You must be drunk to score posts. |
| Anonymous<br>*(no login)* | Not unless I'm invited.    3:13<br>No score for this post. Scoring disabled. You must be drunk to score posts. |
| Anonymous<br>*(no login)* | You make a commitment to your team and work hard together all season, only to leave when they need you the most? Now that's selfish!    3:30<br>No score for this post. Scoring disabled. You must be drunk to score posts. |
| Anonymous<br>*(no login)* | There's more to life than hockey, 3:30. The Cold War is over.    4:01<br>No score for this post. Scoring disabled. You must be drunk to score posts. |
| Anonymous<br>*(no login)* | Where'd they go? Depends if it was a warm destination. Good choice and I'm all for it.  7:10<br>No score for this post. Scoring disabled. You must be drunk to score posts. |
| Anonymous<br>*(no login)* | The kid should be sat when they return, and if the season is over by then, he should start the next season riding the pine.    8:03<br><br>No score for this post. Scoring disabled. You must be drunk to score posts. |

| Anonymous <br> *(no login)* | **Network 55** <br> **Re: Should a kid be allowed to miss** <br> **playoffs to go on vacation cont'd** <br><br> We had a coach last year who bag skated any kid who arrived more than a minute late for practice. When the best player's family went to Florida on vacation (and took the kid with them), the coach went to their house and killed their dog as a way of expressing his displeasure. The whole team stood behind the decision (the manager wanted to kill the cats as well).    10:13 <br> <sub>No score for this post. Scoring disabled. You must be drunk to score posts.</sub> |
|---|---|
| Anonymous <br> *(no login)* | Depends if the kid is any good. If he's bottom 5, you send them vacation brochures and help them pack.    10:30 <br> <sub>No score for this post. Scoring disabled. You must be drunk to score posts.</sub> |
| Anonymous <br> *(no login)* | Sitting is good, and the family should be fined, like in the NHL.    10:40 <br><br><br> <sub>No score for this post. Scoring disabled. You must be drunk to score posts.</sub> |

| | |
|---|---|
| Anonymous<br>*(no login)* | **Network 55**<br>**Re: Should a kid be allowed to miss**<br>**playoffs to go on vacation cont'd**<br><br>How can you stop them?  Ask for their passports at the start of season?  Drive team bus in front of plane?  Kidnap dog (before they leave)?    10:45<br>No score for this post. Scoring disabled. You must be drunk to score posts |
| Anonymous<br>*(no login)* | We don't celebrate our kids' birthdays anymore.  Kids on the team were too scared to come, because it might mean missing a practice.  Even if there was no practice, they were supposed to stay by the phone and wait (in case the coach found last-minute ice).10:47<br>No score for this post. Scoring disabled. You must be drunk to score posts. |
| Anonymous<br>*(no login)* | Same thing in the summer with 3x3.  We weren't allowed to go to the beach!    10:48<br>No score for this post. Scoring disabled. You must be drunk to score posts. |
| Anonymous<br>*(no login)* | Sounds like your kids are having a blast.  Where do we sign up?    10:50<br>No score for this post. Scoring disabled. You must be drunk to score posts. |

| Anonymous<br>*(no login)* | **Network 55**<br>**Re: Should a kid be allowed to miss**<br>**playoffs to go on vacation cont'd**<br><br>Our coach told us we couldn't talk to our kid any more, because our parenting style was "not in line with his coaching philosophy." 11.07<br>No score for this post. Scoring disabled. You must be drunk to score posts. |
|---|---|
| Anonymous<br>*(no login)* | Sounds like a good coach . . .                    11:13<br>No score for this post. Scoring disabled. You must be drunk to score posts. |
| Anonymous<br>*(no login)* | My kid had to miss practice to attend his Grampa Bill's funeral last season. Coach didn't believe me . Told me there was "no way in hell you're going to miss it unless you have a Polaroid of good ol' gramps, arms crossed and the whole bit." I took the picture. What else could I do? My kid's a first-line centre!                    12:02<br>No score for this post. Scoring disabled. You must be drunk to score posts. |
| Anonymous<br>*(no login)* | Definitely, kidnap the dog . . .                    12:05<br><br>No score for this post. Scoring disabled. You must be drunk to score posts. |

| | |
|---|---|
| Anonymous<br>*(no login)* | **Network 55**<br>**What's wrong with 2007 AA's in**<br>**Glendon?**<br><br>No score for this post. Scoring disabled. You must be drunk to score posts. |
| Anonymous<br>*(no login)* | The coach is a definite problem – his kid is under-age and, without a doubt, he's not top 5. The other day, I asked him which way he shoots (I was trying to think of better line combinations to suggest to daddy) and the kid says "reft." He doesn't even know left from right: I would cut him immediately.   7:11<br>No score for this post. Scoring disabled. You must be drunk to score posts. |
| Anonymous<br>*(no login)* | Probably doesn't know his colours either.   7:35<br>No score for this post. Scoring disabled. You must be drunk to score posts. |
| Anonymous<br>*(no login)* | Heard his dad was bed wetter (recently).   8:10<br>No score for this post. Scoring disabled. You must be drunk to score posts. |
| Anonymous<br>*(no login)* | Heard that from kid? Probably meant read better.   8:46<br><br><br>No score for this post. Scoring disabled. You must be drunk to score posts. |

| | |
|---|---|
| Anonymous<br>*(no login)* | **Network 55**<br>**What's wrong with 2007 AA's cont'd**<br><br>But is this Glendon coach any good?    8:54<br><small>No score for this post. Scoring disabled. You must be drunk to score posts.</small> |
| Anonymous<br>*(no login)* | Not paying attention?  His kid said "reft."<br>Time for a change.    9:01<br><small>No score for this post. Scoring disabled. You must be drunk to score posts.</small> |
| Anonymous<br>*(no login)* | Top 5 in coughing up the puck, maybe.    9:31<br><small>No score for this post. Scoring disabled. You must be drunk to score posts.</small> |
| Anonymous<br>*(no login)* | Recently wet bed or you heard recently?   10:15<br><small>No score for this post. Scoring disabled. You must be drunk to score posts.</small> |
| Anonymous<br>*(no login)* | Grammar Girl online again?  We don't need<br>your stinkin' grammar.    10:16<br><small>No score for this post. Scoring disabled. You must be drunk to score posts.</small> |
| Anonymous<br>*(no login)* | Let's stay on topic, 10:16.  We all agree<br>(even those of us who don't live in town and<br>know nothing about this team) that the coach<br>is  a major problem.  What else is wrong?<br>I'm assuming they're not winning?    10:53<br><br><small>No score for this post. Scoring disabled. You must be drunk to score posts.</small> |

| Anonymous *(no login)* | **Network 55**<br>**What's wrong with 2007 AA's cont'd**<br><br>I hear the coach's kid scored 270 points last year – that true?    10:54<br><sub>No score for this post. Scoring disabled. You must be drunk to score posts.</sub> |
|---|---|
| Anonymous *(no login)* | It is true, but how many were assists? I'm so tired of people not passing to my kid. He's wide-open all the time!    10:56<br><sub>No score for this post. Scoring disabled. You must be drunk to score posts.</sub> |
| Anonymous *(no login)* | Wide-open because he's completely behind the play, 10:56.    10:59<br><sub>No score for this post. Scoring disabled. You must be drunk to score posts.</sub> |
| Anonymous *(no login)* | Bob, is this you?    11:00<br><sub>No score for this post. Scoring disabled. You must be drunk to score posts.</sub> |
| Anonymous *(no login)* | No, they're actually the best team in the league – you should have see the complaints last year . . .    11:02<br><sub>No score for this post. Scoring disabled. You must be drunk to score posts.</sub> |
| Anonymous *(no login)* | The meek shall inherit the earth.    11:05<br><br><sub>No score for this post. Scoring disabled. You must be drunk to score posts.</sub> |

| | |
|---|---|
| Anonymous<br>*(no login)* | **Network 55**<br>**What's wrong with 2007 AA's cont'd**<br><br>But they won't win the Cup, buddy — find a different thread to wander through. 11:07<br>No score for this post. Scoring disabled. You must be drunk to score posts. |
| Anonymous<br>*(no login)* | You guys think less of me if I told you I pay the coach for more ice time? 11:09<br>No score for this post. Scoring disabled. You must be drunk to score posts. |
| Anonymous<br>*(no login)* | I don't think you would be the first. It's not a bad thing — at least you're honest. 11:10<br>No score for this post. Scoring disabled. You must be drunk to score posts. |
| Anonymous<br>*(no login)* | I also mow his grass during the summer . . . and feed his cats when they go away. 11:12<br>No score for this post. Scoring disabled. You must be drunk to score posts. |
| Anonymous<br>*(no login)* | Still sounds reasonable. You're probably friends, too, right? 11:14<br>No score for this post. Scoring disabled. You must be drunk to score posts. |
| Anonymous<br>*(no login)* | And, I almost forgot: I gave his wife a job: I pay her 50K to "do my books" — I don't even have any books. 11:15<br><br>No score for this post. Scoring disabled. You must be drunk to score posts. |

| | |
|---|---|
| Anonymous<br>*(no login)* | **Network 55**<br>**What's wrong with 2007 AA's cont'd**<br><br>How bad is your player? 11:20<br>No score for this post. Scoring disabled. You must be drunk to score posts. |
| Anonymous<br>*(no login)* | I usually just bring the coach coffee . . .<br>thought that would be enough. 11:21<br>No score for this post. Scoring disabled. You must be drunk to score posts. |
| Anonymous<br>*(no login)* | You people are terrible – what is this world<br>coming to? 11:30<br>No score for this post. Scoring disabled. You must be drunk to score posts. |
| Anonymous<br>*(no login)* | An end . . . like this thread. 11:32<br>No score for this post. Scoring disabled. You must be drunk to score posts. |
| Anonymous<br>*(no login)* | Heard the coach's wife is ugly.  True? 11:34<br>No score for this post. Scoring disabled. You must be drunk to score posts. |
| Anonymous<br>*(no login)* | Yes, it is true, but what does that have to<br>with his ability to win games?  Not sure I<br>follow. 11:35<br><br><br><br>No score for this post. Scoring disabled. You must be drunk to score posts. |

| | |
|---|---|
| Anonymous<br>*(no login)* | **Network 55**<br>**What's wrong with 2007 AA's cont'd**<br><br>I'm just sayin' . . . if she's not attractive, it might demoralize kids to have to look at her all game.  Maybe keep her in the background (or lost-and-found closet)?  Could you play D with Elephant Man as a partner?   12:02<br><br><small>No score for this post. Scoring disabled. You must be drunk to score posts.</small> |
| Anonymous<br>*(no login)* | Point taken, 12:02.   12:03<br><br><small>No score for this post. Scoring disabled. You must be drunk to score posts.</small> |
| Anonymous<br>*(no login)* | I slept with the coach's wife, too.   12:05<br><br><small>No score for this post. Scoring disabled. You must be drunk to score posts.</small> |
| Anonymous<br>*(no login)* | You again?  What's your issue, 12:05?   12:08<br><br><small>No score for this post. Scoring disabled. You must be drunk to score posts.</small> |
| Anonymous<br>*(no login)* | Bored.  Felt I should volunteer more.   12:10<br><br><small>No score for this post. Scoring disabled. You must be drunk to score posts.</small> |
| Anonymous<br>*(no login)* | You couldn't just fundraise?   1:05<br><br><small>No score for this post. Scoring disabled. You must be drunk to score posts.</small> |

| Anonymous<br>*(no login)* | **Network 55**<br>**When is a good time to pull the goalie?**<br><br>No score for this post. Scoring disabled. You must be drunk to score posts. |
|---|---|
| Anonymous<br>*(no login)* | Before the game even starts. 1:41<br>No score for this post. Scoring disabled. You must be drunk to score posts. |
| Anonymous<br>*(no login)* | OK, goalie dad, what's your problem? 1:56<br>No score for this post. Scoring disabled. You must be drunk to score posts. |
| Anonymous<br>*(no login)* | 7:30 on a Tuesday night. 2:05<br>No score for this post. Scoring disabled. You must be drunk to score posts. |
| Anonymous<br>*(no login)* | Well, it's just that he let in 2 goals and was pulled early in the first last night. 2:08<br>No score for this post. Scoring disabled. You must be drunk to score posts. |
| Anonymous<br>*(no login)* | A good coach will let the goalies and their parents know the "rules" up front. Worst thing you can do is surprise or embarrass people. There's 5 other kids on the ice that can make a difference, but sometimes pulling the goalie is a "wake-up call" for the entire team. It's a tactical move that can lead to an instant momentum shift. 2:10<br><br>No score for this post. Scoring disabled. You must be drunk to score posts. |

| | |
|---|---|
| Anonymous<br>*(no login)* | **Network 55**<br>**When to pull the goalie cont'd**<br><br>Suck it up, buttercup.  Goalies should be thick-skinned . . . like alligators, only above water/ice. 2:31 <br>No score for this post. Scoring disabled. You must be drunk to score posts. |
| Anonymous<br>*(no login)* | Meanwhile, the coach's kid lets in 10 goals and doesn't get pulled, and . . . 2:41 <br>No score for this post. Scoring disabled. You must be drunk to score posts. |
| Anonymous<br>*(no login)* | . . . Hold on, 2:41.  Coach's kid?  My apologies.  Enough said.  Old story.  Wait 'til next season.  New thread, please! 2:42 <br>No score for this post. Scoring disabled. You must be drunk to score posts. |
| Anonymous<br>*(no login)* | What's wrong with our team's goalie? 2:46 <br>No score for this post. Scoring disabled. You must be drunk to score posts. |
| Anonymous<br>*(no login)* | Team name might help here . . . 2:49 <br>No score for this post. Scoring disabled. You must be drunk to score posts. |
| Anonymous<br>*(no login)* | It's just that he just can't seem to stop a beach ball. 3:10 <br><br>No score for this post. Scoring disabled. You must be drunk to score posts. |

| | |
|---|---|
| Anonymous<br>*(no login)* | **Network 5**<br>**When to pull the goalie cont'd**<br><br>It's usually a combination of things. Work on his stance. Maybe his glove is too low? Stick on the ice? Spend as much time as you can shooting more pucks at this kid.  3:12<br><br>No score for this post. Scoring disabled. You must be drunk to score posts. |
| Anonymous<br>*(no login)* | I'm just another hockey dad, 3:12. I can't just shoot pucks at this kid whenever I want. At least, I don't think I can?  3:14<br><br>No score for this post. Scoring disabled. You must be drunk to score posts. |
| Anonymous<br>*(no login)* | I sent the goalie's parents an anonymous email (I signed it "Anonymous," but it came from my email) saying the team would pay for a goalie camp (preferrably one that was held at the same times as our games). There's just too many holes to plug.  3:16<br><br>No score for this post. Scoring disabled. You must be drunk to score posts. |
| Moderator | Let's refrain from talking about specific kids. We know who you're talking about, though. Brutal. My sympathies.  3:17<br>No score for this post. Scoring disabled. You must be drunk to score posts. |

# Post-game Wrap-up

## Take the Crazy
## (Or Just Very Dedicated?)
## Hockey Dad Test*

\* *And you can always just ignore the results.*

1. A good coach is someone who:
   a) builds skill and develops confidence
   b) doesn't play favourites
   c) runs well-planned practices
   d) I have heard about but have never met

2. The thing that upsets me most about the Zamboni driver is:

   a) when he "misses a spot"
   b) when he leaves too much water in our end
   c) when he drives too slowly
   d) all of the above!

3. The best way to get my player more ice time is to:
   a) demand that he play "D"
   b) suggest that we "get a power play going"
   c) hope for some "PK time"
   d) tell him to "stay out there as long as possible"

4. The best way of handling disagreements is to:
   a) talk it out like 2 adults
   b) turn the other cheek
   c) try to look at things from the other person's perspective
   d) look after it "mano a mano"

5. When your team's goalie is going through a slump:
   a) offer encouragement and be positive
   b) keep quiet
   c) remind everyone that "it's a team game"
   d) throw tape balls at the goalie's parents to "see if the problem is hereditary"

6. The people on our Minor Hockey Executive Committee are:
   a) a collection of the best and brightest
   b) to be commended for the late nights and long hours they put in
   c) dedicated to developing all the kids
   d) outside my house right now

7. The young referees on the ice today are:
   a) just kids, and should be "given a break"
   b) doing well for their age
   c) improving and maturing with each game
   d) not dropping the puck fast enough


8. Paying players for goals is:
   a) a way to teach them the value of money.
   b) not a bad move, as long as they are also paid for assists
   c) definitely not something that should be talked about in the dressing room
   d) money that could have gone directly to the coach for extra playing time


9. The last time I was on the ice was to:
   a) skate in the parent/player game
   b) help our coach during practice
   c) take pictures of the team after our big tournament win
   d) discuss a call with the ref

10. When I leave the rink, it is usually to:
    a) go home and relax
    b) do some work around the house
    c) go back to work
    d) go as fast as I can to another rink


11. The extra money we had saved before hockey is:
    a) tucked away for their college education
    b) being saved for a big trip
    c) going against the mortgage
    d) gone


12. The role of my kid's teammates should be to:
    a) support each other
    b) have fun together at tournaments
    c) learn life lessons from hockey
    d) get out of my player's way

# *Test Results*

*Incorrect Answer Keys:*

1. *d*
2. *d*
3. *d . . . seems like a lot of "d"s*
4. *Answers will vary.*
5. *All the answers sound pretty good.*
6. *d*
7. *d*
8. *d*
9. *d*
10. *d*
11. *d*
12. *d*

*If you answered with mostly a's, b's, or c 's (and only the odd "d"), then CONGRATULATIONS, you're not completely crazy — just crazy about your kid.*